It is widely thought, even in Scot
wrote all of his poetry in the Sco....... dialect.

In fact, he wrote over 100 poems in pure English. This
book contains a selection of some of these works.

The poems are exactly as he wrote them. No verses have
been omitted.

"He never touched a sentiment without
carrying it to its ultimate expression, and
leaving nothing further to be said."
Abraham Lincoln on Robert Burns

Dedicated to the memory of
my husband George.

Contents

Poems of a Religious Nature

Autobiographical Poems

Poems About Death

Poems About Nature

Verses Written With A Pencil

OVER THE CHIMNEY-PIECE IN THE PARLOUR OF
THE INN AT KENMORE, TAYMOUTH

Admiring Nature in her wildest grace,
These northern scenes with weary feet I trace;
O'er many a winding dale and painful steep,
Th' abodes of covey'd grouse and timid sheep
My savage journey, curious, I pursue,
Till fam'd Breadalbane opens to my view.
The meeting cliffs each deep-sunk glen divides:
The woods, wild-scatter'd, clothe their ample sides;
Th' outstretching lake, imbosomed 'mong the hills,
The eye with wonder and amazement fills:
The Tay meand'ring sweet in infant pride,
The palace rising on his verdant side,
The lawns wood-fring'd in Nature's native taste,
The hillocks dropt in Nature's careless haste,
The arches striding o'er the new-born stream,
The village glittering in the noontime beam —

Poetic ardors in my bosom swell,
Lone wand'ring by the hermit's mossy cell;
The sweeping theatre of hanging woods,
Th' incessant roar of headlong tumbling floods —

Here Poesy might wake her heav'n-taught lyre,
And look through Nature with creative fire;
Here, to the wrongs of Fate half reconcil'd,
Misfortune's lighten'd steps might wander wild;
And Disappointment , in these lonely bounds,
Find balm to soothe her bitter rankling wounds;
Here heart-struck Grief might heav'nward stretch
    her scan,
And injur'd Worth forget and pardon man.

o O o

The Primrose

1

Dost ask me, why I send thee here
The firstling of the infant year:
This lovely native of the vale,
That hangs so pensive and so pale?

2

Look on its bending stalk, so weak.
That, each way yielding does not break,
And see how aptly it reveals
The doubts and fears a lover feels.

3

Look on its leaves of yellow hue
Bepearl'd thus with morning dew,
And these will whisper in thine ears:—
'The sweets of loves are wash'd with tears'.

o O o

On Scaring Some Water-Fowl
In Loch Turit

A WILD SCENE AMONG THE HILLS OF OUGHTERTYRE

Why, ye tenants of the lake,
For me your wat'ry haunt forsake?
Tell me, fellow creatures, why
At my presence thus you fly?
Why disturb your social joys,
Parent, filial, kindred ties?—

Common friend to you and me,
Nature's gifts to all are free:
Peaceful keep your dimpling wave,
Busy feed, or wanton lave;
Or, beneath the sheltering rock,
Bide the surging billow's shock.

Conscious, blushing for our race,
Soon, too soon, your fears I trace.
Man, your proud, usurping foe,
Would be lord of all below:
Plumes himself in freedom's pride,
Tyrant stern to all beside.

The eagle, from the cliffy brow
Marking you his prey below,
In his breast no pity dwells,
Strong necessity compels:
But Man, to whom alone is giv'n
A ray direct from pitying Heav'n,
Glories in his heart humane—
And creatures for his pleasure slain!

In these savage, liquid plains,
Only known to wand'ring swains,
Where the mossy riv'let strays
Far from human haunts and ways,
All on Nature you depend,
And life's poor season peaceful spend.

Or, if Man's superior might
Dare invade your native right,
On the lofty ether borne,
Man with all his powers you scorn;
Swiftly seek, on clanging wings,
Other lakes, and other springs;
And the foe you cannot brave,
Scorn at least to be his slave.

o O o

Poems About Women/Love

Clarinda, Mistress Of My Soul

1

Clarinda, mistress of my soul,
  The measur'd time is run!
The wretch beneath the dreary pole
  So marks his latest sun.

2

To what dark cave of frozen night
  Shall poor Sylvander hie,
Depriv'd of thee, his life and light,
  The sun of all his joy?

3

We part—but, by these precious drops
  That fill thy lovely eyes,
No other light shall guide my steps
  Till thy bright beams arise!

4

She, the fair sun of all her sex,
  Has blest my glorious day;
And shall a glimmering planet fix
  My worship to its ray?

o O o

Thine Am I

1

Thine am I, my faithful Fair,
  Thine my lovely Nancy!
Ev'ry pulse along my veins,
  Ev'ry roving fancy!
To thy bosom lay my heart
  There to throb and languish.
Tho' despair had wrung its core,
  That would heal its anguish.

2

Take away those rosy lips
  Rich with balmy treasure!
Turn away thine eyes of love,
  Lest I die with pleasure!
What is life when wanting love?
  Night without a morning!
Love the cloudless summer's sun,
  Nature gay adorning.

o O o

Flow Gently Sweet Afton

1

Flow gently, sweet Afton, among thy green braes!
Flow gently, I'll sing thee a song in thy praise!
My Mary's asleep by thy murmuring stream—
Flow gently , sweet Afton, disturb not her dream!

2

Thou stock dove whose echo resounds thro' the glen,
Ye wild whistling blackbirds in yon thorny den,
Thou green-crested lapwing, thy screaming forbear—
I charge you, disturb not my slumbering fair!

3

How lofty, sweet Afton, thy neighbouring hills,
Far mark'd with the courses of clear, winding rills!
There daily I wander, as noon rises high,
My flocks and my Mary's sweet cot in my eye.

4

How pleasant thy banks and green vallies below,
Where wild in the woodlands the primroses blow;
There oft, as mild ev'ning weeps over the lea,
The sweet-scented birch shades my Mary and me.

5

Thy crystal stream, Afton, how lovely it glides,
And winds by the cot where my Mary resides!
How wanton thy waters her snowy feet lave,
As, gathering sweet flowerets, she stems thy clear wave!

6

Flow gently, sweet Afton, among thy green braes!
Flow gently, sweet river, the theme of my lays!
My Mary's asleep by thy murmuring stream—
Flow gently, sweet Afton, disturb not her dream!

o O o

The Belles Of Mauchline

1

In Mauchline there dwells six proper young belles,
The pride of the place and its neighbourhood a',
Their carriage and dress, a stranger would guess,
In Lon'on or Paris they'd gotten it a'.

2

Miss Millar is fine, Miss Markland's divine,
Miss Smith she has wit, and Miss Betty is braw,
There's beauty and fortune to get wi' Miss Morton;
But Armour's the jewel for me o' them a'.

(He married Jean Armour)

o O o

To An Old Sweetheart

WRITTEN ON A COPY OF HIS POEMS

1

Once fondly lov'd and still remember'd dear,
  Sweet early object of my youthful vows,
Accept this mark of friendship, warm, sincere—
  (Friendship! 'tis all cold duty now allows);

2

And when you read the simple artless rhymes,
  One friendly sigh for him—he asks no more—
Who, distant, burns in flaming torrid climes,
  Or haply lies beneath th' Atlantic roar.

o O o

It Was The Charming Month Of May

1

It was the charming month of May,
When all the flow'rs were fresh and gay,
One morning, by the break of day,
The youthful, charming Chloe!
From peaceful slumber she arose,
Girt on her mantle and her hose,
And o'er the flow'ry mead she goes—
The youthful, charming Chloe!

2

The feather'd people you might see
Perch'd all around on every tree!
With notes of sweetest melody
They hail the charming Chloe,
Till, painting gay the eastern skies,
The glorious sun began to rise,
Outrival'd by the radiant eyes
Of youthful charming Chloe.

o O o

Young Peggy

1

Young Peggy blooms our bonniest lass:
  Her blush is like the morning,
The rosy dawn the springing grass
  With early gems adorning;
Her eyes outshine the radiant beams
  That gild the passing shower,
And glitter o'er the crystal streams,
  And cheer each fresh'ning flower.

2

Her lips, more than the cherries bright—
  A richer dye has graced them—
They charm the admiring gazer's sight,
  And sweetly tempt to taste them.
Her smile is as the evening mild,
  When feather'd pairs are courting,
And little lambkins wanton wild,
  In playful bands disporting.

3

Were Fortune lovely Peggy's foe,
Such sweetness would relent her:
As blooming Spring unbends the brow
Of surly, savage Winter.
Detraction's eye no aim can gain
Her winning powers to lessen,
And fretful Envy grins in vain
The poison'd tooth to fasten.

4

Ye Pow'rs of Honour, Love, and Truth,
From ev'ry ill defend her!
Inspire the highly-favour'd youth
 The destinies intend her!
Still fan the sweet connubial flame
Responsive in each bosom,
And bless the dear parental name
 With many a filial blossom!

o O o

Where, Braving Angry Winter's Storms

1

Where, braving angry winter's storms,
The lofty Ochils rise,
Far in their shade my Peggy's charms
First blest my wondering eyes:
As one who by some savage stream
A lonely gem surveys,
Astonish'd doubly, marks it beam
With art's most polish'd blaze.

2

Blest be the wild, sequester'd glade,
And blest the day and hour,
Where Peggy's charms I first survey'd,
When first I felt their pow'r!
The tyrant death with grim control
May seize my fleeting breath,
But tearing Peggy from my soul
Must be a stronger death.

o O o

On Marriage

That hackney'd judge of human life,
 The Preacher and the King,
Observes:— 'The man that gets a wife
He gets a noble thing.'
But how capricious are mankind,
Now loathing, now desirous!
We married men, how oft we find
The best of things will tire us!

o O o

On A Bank Of Flowers

1

On a bank of flowers in a summer day,
For summer lightly drest,
The blooming youthful Nelly lay
 With love and sleep opprest;
When Willie, wand'ring thro' the wood,
Who for her favour oft had sued—
He gaz'd, he wish'd,
He fear'd, he blush'd,
And trembled where he stood.

2

Her closèd eyes, like weapons sheath'd,
Were seal'd in soft repose;
Her lips, still as she fragrant breath'd,
It richer dyed the rose;
The springing lilies, sweetly prest,
Wild-wanton kiss'd her rival breast:
He gaz'd, he wish'd,
He fear'd, he blush'd,
His bosom ill at rest.

3

Her robes, light-waving in the breeze,
Her tender limbs embrace;
Her lovely form, her native ease,
All harmony and grace.
Tumultuous tides his pulses roll,
A faltering, ardent kiss he stole:
He gaz'd, he wish'd,
He fear'd, he blush'd,
And sigh'd his very soul.

4

As flies the partridge from the break
On fear enspirèd wings,
So Nelly starting, half-awake,
Away affrighted springs.
But Willie follow'd—as he should;
He overtook her in the wood;
He vow'd, he pray'd,
He found the maid
Forgiving all, and good.

o O o

Bonnie Bell

1

The smiling Spring comes in rejoicing,
And surly Winter grimly flies.
Now crystal clear are the falling waters,
And bonny blue are the sunny skies.
Fresh o'er the mountains breaks forth the morning,
The ev'ning gilds the ocean's swell:
All creatures joy in the sun's returning,
And I rejoice in my bonnie Bell.

2

The flowery Spring leads sunny Summer,
The yellow Autumn presses near;
Then in his turn comes gloomy Winter,
Till smiling Spring again appear.
Thus seasons dancing, life advancing,
Old Time and Nature their changes tell;
But never ranging, still unchanging,
I adore my bonnie Bell.

o O o

From Thee Eliza

1

From thee Eliza, I must go,
And from my native shore:
The cruel fates between us throw
A boundless ocean's roar;
But boundless oceans, roaring wide
Between my love and me,
They never, never can divide
My heart and soul from thee.

2

Farewell, farewell, Eliza dear,
The maid that I adore!
A boding voice is in mine ear,
 We part to meet no more!
But the latest throb that leaves my heart,
While Death stands victor by,
That throb, Eliza, is thy part,
And thine that latest sigh!

o O o

Poems Giving Advice

Verses In Friar's Carse Hermitage

Thou whom chance may hither lead,
Be thou clad in russet weed,
Be thou deck'd in silken stole,
Grave these counsels on thy soul: —

Life is but a day at most,
Sprung from night in darkness lost;
Hope not sunshine every hour,
Fear not clouds will always lour.
Happiness is but a name,
Make content and ease thy aim.
Ambition is a meteor-gleam;
Fame a restless airy dream;
Pleasures, insects on the wing
Round Peace, th' tend'rest flow'r of spring;
Those that sip the dew alone—
Make the butterflies thy own;

Those that would the bloom devour—
Crush the locusts, save the flower.
For the future be prepar'd:
Guard wherever thou can'st guard;
But, thy utmost duly done,
Welcome what thou can'st not shun.
Follies past give thou to air—
Make their consequence thy care.
Keep the name of man in mind,
And dishonour not thy kind.
Reverence with lowly heart
Him, whose wondrous work thou art;
Keep His Goodness still in view—
Thy trust, and thy example too.

Stranger, go! Heaven be thy guide!
Quod the Beadsman on Nidside.

o O o

Strathallan's Lament

1

Thickest night, surround my dwelling!
Howling tempests, o'er me rave!
Turbid torrents wintry-swelling,
Roaring by my lonely cave!
Crystal streamlets gently flowing,
Busy haunts of base mankind,
Western breezes softly blowing,
Suit not my distracted mind.

2

In the cause of Right engagèd,
Wrongs injurious to redress,
Honour's war we strongly wagèd,
But the heavens denied success.
Ruin's wheel has driven o'er us:
Not a hope that dare attend,
The wide world is all before us,
But a world without a friend.

o O o

Man Was Made To Mourn

A DIRGE

1

When chill November's surly blast
Made fields and forests bare,
One ev'ning, as I wand'red forth
Along the banks of Ayr,
I spied a man, whose agèd step
Seem'd weary, worn with care,
His face was furrow'd o'er with years,
And hoary was his hair.

2

'Young stranger, whither wand'rest thou?'
Began the rev'rend Sage;
'Does thirst of wealth thy step constrain,
Or youthful pleasure's rage?
Or haply, prest with cares and woes,
Too soon thou hast began
To wander forth, with me to mourn
The miseries of Man.

3

'The sun that overhangs yon moors,
Out-spreading far and wide,
Where hundreds labour to support
A haughty lordling's pride:
I've seen yon weary winter-sun
Twice forty times return;
And ev'ry time has added proofs,
That Man was made to mourn.

4

'O Man! while in thy early years,
How prodigal of time!
Mis-spending all thy precious hours,
Thy glorious, youthful prime!
Alternate follies take the sway,
Licentious passions burn:
Which tenfold force gives Nature's law,
That Man was made to mourn.

5

'Look not alone on youthful prime,
Or manhood's active might;
Man then is useful to his kind,
Supported is his right:
But see him on the edge of life,
With cares and sorrows worn;
Then Age and Want—O ill-match'd pair! —
Shew Man was made to mourn.

6

'A few seem favourites of Fate,
In Pleasure's lap carest;
Yet think not all the rich and great
Are likewise truly blest:
But oh! what crowds in ev'ry land,
All wretched and forlorn,
Thro' weary life this lesson learn,
That Man was made to mourn.

7

'Many and sharp the num'rous ills
Inwoven with our frame!
More pointed still we make ourselves
Regret, remorse, and shame!
And Man, whose heav'n-erected face
The smiles of love adorn,—
Man's inhumanity to man
Makes countless thousands mourn!

8

'See yonder poor, o'erlabour'd wight,
So abject, mean, and vile,
Who begs a brother of the earth
To give him leave to toil;
And see his lordly fellow-worm
The poor petition spurn,
Unmindful, tho' a weeping wife
And helpless offspring mourn.

9

'If I'm design'd yon lordling's slave—
By Nature's law design'd—
Why was an independent wish
E'er planted in my mind?
If not, why am I subject to
His cruelty, or scorn?
Or why has Man the will and pow'r
To make his fellow mourn?

10

'Yet let not this too much, my son,
Disturb thy youthful breast:
This partial view of human-kind
Is surely not the last!
The poor, oppressèd, honest man
Had never, sure, been born,
Had there not been some recompense
To comfort those that mourn!

11

'O Death! the poor man's dearest friend,
The kindest and the best!
Welcome the hour my agèd limbs
 Are laid with thee at rest!
The great, the wealthy fear thy blow,
From pomp and pleasure torn;
But, oh! a blest relief to those
That weary-laden mourn!'

o O o

Poems Of A Religious Nature

Prayer Under The Pressure Of Violent Anguish

1

O Thou Great Being! what Thou art
Surpasses me to know;
Yet sure I am, that known to Thee
Are all Thy works below.

2

Thy creature here before Thee stands,
All wretched and distrest;
Yet sure those ills that wring my soul
Obey Thy high behest.

3

Sure, Thou, Almighty, canst not act
From cruelty or wrath!
O, free my weary eyes from tears,
Or close them fast in death!

4

But if I must afflicted be
To suit some wise design,
Then man my soul with firm resolves
To bear and not repine!

o O o

Paraphrase Of The First Psalm

1

The man, in life wherever plac'd,
Hath happiness in store,
Who walks not in the wicked's way
Nor learns their guilty lore.

2

Nor from the seat of scornful pride
Casts forth his eyes abroad,
But with humility and awe
Still walks before his God!

3

That man shall flourish like the trees,
Which by the streamlets grow:
The fruitful top is spread on high,
And firm the root below.

4

But he, whose blossom buds in guilt,
Shall to the ground be cast,
And, like the rootless stubble, tost
Before the sweeping blast.

5

For why? that God the good adore
Hath giv'n them peace and rest,
But hath decreed that wicked men
Shall ne'er be truly blest.

o O o

Autobiographical Poems

My Father Was A Farmer

1

My father was a farmer upon the Carrick border, O,
And carefully he bred me in decency and order, O.
He bade me act a manly part, though I had ne'er a farthing, O,
For without an honest, manly heart no man was worth
   regarding, O.

2

Then out into the world my course I did determine, O:
Tho' to be rich was not my wish, yet to be great was
   charming, O.
My talents they were not the worst, nor yet my education,
   O—
Resolv'd was I at least to try to mend my situation,
   O.

3

In many a way and vain essay I courted Fortune's favour, O:
Some cause unseen still stept between to frustrate each
  endeavour, O.
Sometimes by foes I was o'erpower'd, sometimes by friends
  forsaken, O,
And when my hope was at the top, I still was worst mistaken,
  O.

4

Then sore harass'd, and tir'd at last with Fortune's vain
  delusion, O,
I dropt my schemes like idle dreams, and came to this
  conclusion, O:—
The past was bad, and the future hid; its good or ill untried,
  O,
But the present hour was in my pow'r, and so I would enjoy
  it, O.

5

No help, nor hope, nor view had I, nor person to befriend me,
  O;
So I must toil, and sweat, and broil, and labour to sustain me,
  O!
To plough and sow, to reap and mow, my father bred me early,
  O:
For one, he said, to labour bred was a match for Fortune fairly,
  O.

6

Thus all obscure, unknown, and poor, thro' life I'm doom'd to
  wander, O,
Till down my weary bones I lay in everlasting slumber, O.
No view nor care, but shun whate'er might breed me pain or
  sorrow, O,
I live to-day as well's I may, regardless of to-morrow, O!

7

But, cheerful still, I am as well as a monarch in a palace, O,
Tho' Fortune's frown still hunts me down, with all her wonted
   malice, O:
I make indeed my daily bread, but ne'er can make it farther, O,
But, as daily bread is all I need, I do not much regard her, O.

8

When sometimes by my labour I earn a little money, O,
Some unforeseen misfortune comes gen'rally upon me, O:
Mischance, mistake, or by neglect, or my good-natur'd folly,
   O—
But come what will, I've sworn it still, I'll ne'er be
melancholy, O.

9

All you who follow wealth and power with unremitting
   ardour, O,
The more in this you look for bliss, you leave your view the
   farther, O.
Had you the wealth Potosi boasts, or nations to adore you, O,
A cheerful, honest-hearted clown I will prefer before you, O!

o O o

The Gloomy Night Is Gathering Fast

1

The gloomy night is gath'ring fast,
Loud roars the wild inconstant blast;
Yon murky cloud is filled with rain,
I see it driving o'er the plain;
The hunter now has left the moor,
The scatt'red coveys meet secure;
While here I wander prest with care,
Along the lonely banks of Ayr.

2

The Autumn mourns her rip'ning corn
By early Winter's ravage torn;
Across her placid, azure sky,
She sees the scowling tempest fly;
Chill runs my blood to hear it rave:
I think upon the stormy wave,
Where many a danger I must dare,
Far from the bonnie banks of Ayr.

3

'Tis not the surging billows' roar,
'Tis not that fatal deadly shore;
Tho' death in ev'ry shape appear,
The wretched have no more to fear:
But round my heart the ties are bound,
That heart transpierc'd with many a wound;
These bleed afresh, those ties I tear,
To leave the bonnie banks of Ayr.

4

Farewell old Coila's hills and dales,
Her heathy moors and winding vales;
The scenes where wretched Fancy roves,
Pursuing past unhappy loves!
Farewell my friends! farewell my foes!
My peace with these, my love with those—
The bursting tears my heart declare,
Farewell my bonnie banks of Ayr.

o O o

The Lazy Mist

1

The lazy mist hangs from the brow of the hill,
Concealing the course of the dark winding rill.
How languid the scenes, late so sprightly, appear,
As Autumn to Winter resigns the pale year!

2

The forests are leafless, the meadows are brown,
And all the gay foppery of summer is flown.
Apart let me wander, apart let me muse,
How quick Time is flying, how keen Fate pursues!

3

How long have I liv'd, but how much liv'd in vain!
How little of life's scanty span may remain!
What aspects old Time in his progress has worn!
What ties cruel Fate in my bosom has torn!

4

How foolish, or worse, till our summit is gain'd!
And downward, how weaken'd, how darken'd, how pain'd!
Life is not worth having with all it can give:
For something beyond it poor man, sure, must live.

o O o

Poems About Death

A Prayer In The Prospect Of Death

1
O Thou unknown, Almighty Cause
Of all my hope and fear!
In whose dread presence, ere an hour,
Perhaps I must appear!

2
If I have wander'd in those paths
Of life I ought to shun—
As something, loudly, in my breast,
Remonstrates I have done—

3
Thou know'st that Thou hast form̀ed me
With passions wild and strong;
And list'ning to their witching voice
Has often led me wrong.

4
Where human weakness has come short,
Or frailty stept aside'
Do Thou, All-good—for such Thou art—
In shades of darkness hide.

5
Where with intention I have err'd'
No other plea I have,
But, Thou art good; and Goodness still
Delighteth to forgive.

o O o

On Wm. Muir In Tarbolton Mill

An honest man here lies at rest,
As e'er God with His image blest:
The friend of man, the friend of truth,
The friend of age, and guide of youth:
Few hearts like his—with virtue warm'd,
Few heads with knowledge so inform'd:
If there's another world, he lives in bliss;
If there is none, he made the best of this.

o O o

For Mr. Walter Riddell

So vile was poor Wat, such a miscreant slave,
That the worms ev'n damn'd him when laid in his grave.
'In his skull there's a famine,' a starved reptile cries;
'And his heart, it is poison,' another replies.

o O o

On Reading In A Newspaper
The Death Of John M'leod, Esq.

BROTHER TO A YOUNG LADY,

A PARTICULAR FRIEND OF THE AUTHOR'S

1

Sad thy tale, thou idle page,
And rueful thy alarms:
Death tears the brother of her love
From Isabella's arms.

2

Sweetly deckt with pearly dew
The morning rose may blow;
But cold successive noontide blasts
May lay its beauties low.

3

Fair on Isabella's morn
The sun propitious smil'd;
But, long ere noon, succeeding clouds
Succeeding hopes beguil'd.

4

Fate oft tears the bosom-chords
That Nature finest strung:
So Isabella's heart was form'd,
And so that heart was wrung.

5

Dread Omnipotence alone
Can heal the wound he gave—
Can point the brimful, grief-worn eyes
To scenes beyond the grave.

6

Virtue's blossoms there shall blow,
And fear no withering blast;
There Isabella's spotless worth
Shall happy be at last.

o O o

Thou Lingering Star

1

Thou ling'ring star with less'ning ray,
That lov'st to greet the early morn,
Again thou usher'st in the day
My Mary from my soul was torn.
O Mary, dear departed shade!
Where is thy place of blissful rest?
See'st thou thy lover lowly laid?
Hear'st thou the groans that rend his breast?

2

That sacred hour can I forget,
Can I forget the hallow'd grove,
Where, by the winding Ayr, we met
To live one day of parting love?
Eternity cannot efface
Those records dear of transports past,
Thy image at our last embrace—
Ah! little thought we 'twas our last!

3

Ayr, gurgling, kiss'd his pebbled shore,
O'erhung with wild woods thickening green;
The fragrant birch and hawthorne hoar
Twin'd amorous round the raptur'd scene;
The flowers sprang wanton to be prest,
The birds sang love on every spray,
Till too, too soon, the glowing west
Proclaim'd the speed of wingèd day.

4

Still o'er these scenes my mem'ry wakes,
And fondly broods with miser-care.
Time but th' impression stronger makes,
As streams their channels deeper wear.
O Mary, dear departed shade!
 Where is thy place of blissful rest?
See'st thou thy lover lowly laid?
Hear'st thou the groans that rend his breast?

o O o

For The Author's Father

ENGRAVED ON THE HEADSTONE OF ROBERT BURNS'
FATHER IN THE KIRKYARD AT ALLOWAY, NEAR AYR.

O ye whose cheek the tear of pity stains,
Draw near with pious rev'rence, and attend!
Here lie the loving husband's dear remains,
The tender father, and the gen'rous friend.

The pitying heart that felt for human woe,
The dauntless heart that fear'd no human pride,
The friend of man—to vice alone a foe;
For "ev'n his failings lean'd to virtue's side".

o O o